The School Rules

RULES AT LUNCH

By Paul Bloom

Gareth Stevens
PUBLISHING

Please visit our website, www.garethstevens.com. For a free color catalog of all our high-quality books, call toll free 1-800-542-2595 or fax 1-877-542-2596.

Library of Congress Cataloging-in-Publication Data

Bloom, Paul.
Rules at lunch / by Paul Bloom.
p. cm. — (The school rules)
Includes index.
ISBN 978-1-4824-2637-3 (pbk.)
ISBN 978-1-4824-2638-0 (6 pack)
ISBN 978-1-4824-2639-7 (library binding)
1. School children — Food — Juvenile literature. 2. School children — Juvenile literature. I. Bloom, Paul, 1963-. II. Title.
LB3475.B56 2016
371.7′16—d23

First Edition

Published in 2016 by
Gareth Stevens Publishing
111 East 14th Street, Suite 349
New York, NY 10003

Copyright © 2016 Gareth Stevens Publishing

Editor: Ryan Nagelhout
Designer: Laura Bowen

Photo credits: Cover, p. 1 (main children) Tetra Images - Jamie Grill/Brand X Pictures/Getty Images; cover, p. 1 (background children) Pressmaster/Shutterstock.com; cover, p. 1 (classroom background) archideaphoto/Shutterstock.com; p. 5 Rob Lewine/Getty Images; pp. 7, 24 (cafeteria) hxdbzxy/ Shutterstock.com; pp. 9, 17 Monkey Business Images/Shutterstock.com; p. 11 © iStockphoto.com/SolStock; p. 13 © iStockphoto.com/omgimages; p. 15 Olesya Feketa/Shutterstock.com; pp. 19, 23 Kidstock/ Blend Images/Getty Images; pp. 21, 24 (waste) GreenLookPook/Shutterstock.com.

All rights reserved. No part of this book may be reproduced in any form without permission in writing from the publisher, except by a reviewer.

Printed in the United States of America

CPSIA compliance information: Batch #CS15GS: For further information contact Gareth Stevens, New York, New York at 1-800-542-2595.

Contents

I'm hungry!
It's time for lunch.

I eat lunch
in a big room.
This is called
a cafeteria.

You have to follow the rules at lunch.

It's fun to eat
with friends.

Don't take food
from them.

13

Don't throw any food!

Try not to spill your drink.

Clean up after you are done eating.

Throw away any waste.

21

You can help your
friends clean up, too!

Words to Know

cafeteria

waste

Index